Today I Will Nourish My Inner Martyr

ANN THORNHILL & SARAH WELLS

Today I Will

Nourish My

Inner Martyr

AFFIRMATIONS FOR CYNICS

PRIMA PUBLISHING

PRIMA PUBLISHING and colophon are registered trademarks of Prima Communications, Inc.

Library of Congress Cataloging-in-Publication Data

Wells, Sarah.
    Today I will nourish my inner martyr: affirmations for cynics / Sarah Wells and Ann Thornhill.
        p.   cm.
    ISBN 0-7615-1423-6
    1. Affirmations–Humor. I. Thornhill, Ann.
PN6231.A42W45 1998
818'.5402–DC21   98-4985
                                                                          CIP

        00 01 02 HH 10 9 8 7 6 5 4
Printed in the United States of America

How to Order

Single copies may be ordered from Prima Publishing, P.O. Box 1260BK, Rocklin, CA 95677; telephone (800) 632-8676. Quantity discounts are also available. On your letterhead, include information concerning the intended use of the books and the number of books you wish to purchase.

Visit us online at www.primapublishing.com

To our dear friends and family members
who have helped us through such hard times
and whose names happen to escape us
at the moment.

Are you as sick of all this pop-psychology, new age advice as we are? Do you get stabbing pains in the gut every time you hear the words *dysfunctional, co-dependent* or *inner-child?* Do book titles like *Single Has-Been Actors and the Tenured University Professors Who Love Them* make your head throb and your vision blur?

If you answered "yes" to any of these questions, then we have the answer. This book is dedicated to everyone who has even one ounce of rebellion left. This book is for everyone who is sick and tired of dishing out money every week to a therapist. This book is a proclamation, a declaration, a provocation; it says, "Hell, I'm a bitter mean-spirited person, and I'm damn proud of it." It says, "I'm number one and no one else even comes close." Or, depending on the day, "I'm nothing; therefore, I deserve nothing." In short, this book has something for each and every one of us.

So sit back and let the transforming energy of anger, revenge, remorse, and self pity fill your soul.

$\mathcal{O}$n this day I will look at my past
mistakes and project them
onto the future.

$\mathcal{T}$oday I will create a crisis situation so I
can feel really alive.

I have a right to be physically unattractive.

❧

I will make spiritual bankruptcy my goal for the day.

$\mathcal{I}$ have a right to change people into
who I want them to be.

❧

$\mathcal{T}$oday I will belittle those around me as
I've been belittled in the past.

Extreme mood swings are my goal for the day, as they are so invigorating.

I have a right to seek revenge on those who have hurt me, and so today I'll begin to intricately plot against them.

$\mathcal{T}$oday I will surround myself with
unhealthy people so that I may
feel superior to them.

∞

$\mathcal{T}$oday I celebrate the fact that my
underdeveloped sense of identity allows
me to fit into a wide range of situations.

Today I will only do things for which
I receive very clear approval or applause.

My choices are limited;
therefore, I must rigidly stick to the
plan I have outlined for myself.

Today I will start a project
only so I can later abandon it because
of my perfectionistic standards.

⁂

Today I will lie in bed and wallow
in self-pity.

$\mathcal{T}$oday I will purposefully fuel
someone's worst fears.

$\mathcal{S}$

$\mathcal{W}$hile in conversations today, I will
practice keeping a mental inventory of
other people's stupidity.

Today I will practice playing the victim
with my friends and coworkers.

❧

This year I will save money
by not buying birthday cards for anyone;
I will tell everyone their card must have
been lost in the mail.

I have the hardest life.

Today I will hoard something I was denied as a child.

It's better to gripe about people behind their backs than to cause problems by confronting them.

Today I will intentionally steal someone's thunder.

My need for closure
makes it okay for me to oversimplify
and pigeonhole everything.

One of my goals for the year will be
complete independence from everyone,
and on all levels.

$\mathcal{T}$oday I will provoke a loved one's anger just to assure myself that I still have an effect on him or her.

$\mathcal{I}$ have a right to use bribery to get my needs met.

My family, friends, and associates
could save me a lot of precious time
by accepting the reality that
I'm always right.

Tonight I will clandestinely shovel
the snow from my walk onto
my neighbor's walk.

I have a right to be dysfunctional.

❧

Today I will acknowledge
my right to thrive in chaos and
panic in tranquility.

Today I will nourish my inner martyr.

⚮

My narcissism will guide me effortlessly through this day.

$\mathcal{T}$oday I will attend a support group or
meeting using an alias.

❧

$\mathcal{I}$ have a right to complain loudly
about fictitious physical symptoms to
elicit sympathy from others.

Today I will buy high-watt light bulbs
for my bathroom so I can better
obsess over my wrinkles.

Of all the seasons,
winter best symbolizes my spirituality—
dead and shriveled.

Today I will practice keeping secrets
from loved ones.

∽

Today I will play mind games
with my therapist.

Today I will remind myself
that my friends and family are just
waiting for me to fail.

❦

Today I will perform self-obsessive
actions, such as making noise
while others try to rest.

Other people create boundaries
only to shut me out.

&

Today I will consciously repeat
a destructive pattern from my past.

When I look at my children today,
I will remind myself that they are
the perfect vehicles through which to
live vicariously.

I will remain tense all day.

Today I will make my significant other
mind-read my feelings.

❧

I am ashamed of who I am;
therefore, I will pretend to be someone
else today.

$\mathcal{P}$eople must all grieve as I do—
silently and privately.

❧

$\mathcal{T}$oday I will make decisions based on my
sense of impending doom.

Since I don't have the right to say, "I don't know," I will pretend to know everything today.

❧

I acknowledge that winter's darkness traps me in my house.

Today I will let my internal anger
guide my actions.

❧

Today I will pretend that everyone I see
is judging me.

. 26 .

I am incompetent.

❧

I have a right to cheat in order to
satisfy my competitive nature.

Although everyone pretends
not to realize it, they know
I am superior to them.

I will ignore my needs today.

Today I will tell a fantastic lie so I can
be the center of attention.

❧

To amuse myself at work today,
I will sneak around and steal
office supplies.

Today, instead of dealing with situations that upset me, I will create melodramatic diversions.

Today I will practice saying "no" at inappropriate times to inappropriate people.

I accept that others control
my happiness.

❧

Today I will be inconsistent and
unpredictable at work.

$\mathcal{M}$y possessions are the only measure
of my success.

✺

$\mathcal{I}$t's better to make a disastrous mess of
something than to ask for help.

$\mathcal{F}$un is for children.
As an adult it is my right to
not have fun.

❧

$\mathcal{H}$obbies are only petty distractions
from the agenda of life.

I will try to consistently
avoid situations in which I cannot excel.

∽

Today I will praise myself for nothing.

$\mathcal{I}$ understand that I have no successes;
therefore, I will work on denying
all my failures.

$\mathcal{T}$oday I will hang up on someone when
the conversation bores me; later, I will
say the phone inexplicably disconnected.

I must remember never to expose
my family by telling anyone
our history.

✍

Today I will pit two of my friends
against each other.

Today I will purchase at least
one product that wreaks havoc
on the environment.

❦

If I feel left out of a conversation today,
I will skillfully draw attention to myself
by saying something rude.

Today I celebrate my ability
to verbally support others while mentally
judging them.

I am entitled to everything I want.

$\mathcal{I}$ am entitled to everything I want,
even if it is someone else's.

❧

$\mathcal{I}$ am entitled to everything I want,
even if it is someone else's and even if
I already have it.

Today I will yawn and fidget
when people try to engage me
in conversation.

Spring's rebirth provides a contrast for
my completely stagnant life.

At least I can take comfort in
the fact that no one knows the real
source of my shame.

Today I will use big words to
intimidate people.

Today I will misuse big words to test other people's intelligence.

Today I will remind myself that it takes a lot of energy to be as dysfunctional as I am; therefore, I deserve rest and physical pampering.

Even the most challenging things
should come easy for me; if they don't,
it's best for me to give up.

Today I will estimate the amount of
time before my next high-school
reunion. Then I will plan the many ways
I can perfect myself before then.

As a child I was expected to be quiet and proper. Today I allow myself to explore loud and obnoxious behaviors.

It shows weakness to change one's opinion about something or someone.

$\mathcal{I}$f I can't sleep tonight, I won't be able to function tomorrow—insomnia is incapacitating. If I can't sleep tonight . . . (repeat incessantly).

⁓

$\mathcal{S}$ometimes problems disappear if they are thoroughly ignored long enough.

Because I unfairly demand too much
from myself, today I allow myself to
act in distinctly untrustworthy and
irresponsible ways.

Today I will play devil's advocate
simply to annoy someone.

This month I will experiment with new medications that effectively mask all my stress-related illnesses.

❦

Because I know what's best for other people, I will spend today solving my friends' problems.

Today I will cultivate a relationship
with an especially needy person so I can
fulfill my need to be needed.

I am surrounded by idiots.

$\mathcal{T}$oday I will practice
my "all-or-nothing" thinking.

❧

$\mathcal{T}$here is no room in my life
for my inner child.

Today I affirm my right to
be fragmented and out of touch.

❦

My recovery is probably not
going anywhere.

Food is the only stable thing in my life;
I embrace it.

❧

Today I will stand naked in front
of a mirror and concentrate on
my physical flaws.

The best years of my life are over.
They weren't exactly good years, but
nonetheless, they are over.

It is okay to have no faith in anything.

Unlike me, the seasons of the year
serve a purpose.

❧

Today I will develop a new, unhealthy
communication technique.

Today I will expect others to anticipate my needs; I will get inappropriately angry if they fail to do so.

Today I will act ambivalently toward my best friend.

I accept that without television,
I would have no new friends.

❧

Whenever I am unfulfilled sexually,
I must remember to blame it
on my partner.

$\mathcal{T}$oday I will give someone the silent treatment and see how long it takes for him or her to notice.

$\mathcal{I}$ will laugh at someone in pain today.

Today I will purposely inconvenience
as many people as I can.

❧

Today I will give unsolicited advice
to those who, in my opinion,
need to better themselves.

Today I will dwell on the ways in
which my parents neglected me.

Instead of being abandoned,
I will abandon someone today.

$\mathcal{I}$t is my inalienable right to wreak havoc in the lives of people I know.

⚬⚬

$\mathcal{I}$ acknowledge my need to manipulate my family.

$\mathcal{I}$t is impossible to raise perfectly
well-adjusted children; therefore, I won't
even try to improve my parenting skills.

$\mathcal{B}$ecause I cannot get any closure from
my childhood pain, I will use blame and
resentment to liberate myself.

I have a right to be emotionally detached from all things around me.

☙

Today I will nurture feelings of helplessness and regret.

I will wear my wounds on
my sleeve today.

My fatigue is eternal.

Guilt will be the driving force
behind my actions today.

Today I will accept that
I feel claustrophobic because I
actually am trapped.

$\mathcal{R}$egardless of what other people say, my tendency to overreact and lose all perspective makes me a theatrically interesting person.

$\mathcal{T}$oday I will question my own confusion.

I will be self-destructive today.

❧

Today I accept and affirm my
bitter disposition.

Today I will do something unethical
just to buck the system.

❧

My anger is the only thing that
makes me powerful.

I have a right to project my own
inadequacies onto other people.

∞

My perceptions are worthless
and misleading.

Today I will make a desperate and
impulsive decision.

❧

I have a right to be overly critical
of others.

$\mathcal{B}$ecause I've had a hard life,
it is okay for me to use name-calling as a
primary means of communication.

❧

$\mathcal{I}$ hate my job, but I am unworthy
of anything better.

Today, instead of taking a nap,
I will lie in bed and make a mental list
of all my shortcomings.

The world will someday realize the
hidden genius of my work.

Everyone should change
their schedules to accommodate me.

*

I must repress my sexual desires.

$\mathcal{I}$ accept myself for what I am—
a materialistically driven charlatan.

❦

$\mathcal{T}$o compensate for my inherent
weakness, I shall surround myself with
controlling people.

Today I will force myself to eat alone at a restaurant; I will then give myself indigestion because I feel so self-conscious and conspicuous.

Today I will encourage others to dismiss my needs and emotions.

Today I will seek out an abusive environment for myself.

I approve of nothing and no one.

Today I will take no responsibility
for anything.

❧

The world is a dangerous place—perhaps
I should stay inside as much as possible.

Control is the only thing
any of us have; therefore, I must hold
on to it at all costs.

My self-doubts are actually perceptive
insights, not the baseless worries that my
therapist tries to trick me into believing.

Today I will escalate my
negative self-talk.

⌘

I am an adult child of
complete children.

Fooling those around me is more
important than doing actual work
toward my own recovery.

Unconditional love should be
reserved for one's pets.

I have no issues.

❧

I will use what little creativity I have
to cultivate new and more original
stress-related illnesses.

Today I will compulsively weigh myself
every hour, each time sinking deeper
into a pool of depression.

Today I will further solidify the
separation between my mind and body.

I must hurry, hurry, hurry to live my life. The future looks bleak.

❧

$Team$ playing is for insecure people who aren't capable of doing things on their own.

So that I can later bore my friends with slides from my fantastic summer vacation, I will go to every tourist trap within driving distance.

If I act incompetent, other people will take care of me.

Today I will read a magazine or book
while someone is communicating their
emotional needs to me.

I remind myself today that sex really
does equal love.

The next time I have insomnia, I will
crank call someone who has hurt me.

❧

Today I will pretend that I am famous
and that everyone I see is a shy,
but adoring fan.

$\mathcal{T}$oday I will be derisive toward
someone who is trying to be helpful.

❧

$\mathcal{T}$oday I will think about how much
more my siblings got than I did.

Today I will remember a disastrous
past adventure and use it as a reason to
not try anything new.

Today I will look at my shortcomings
for what they are—my parents' fault.

As a child, I became an expert at hiding my feelings. Today I will hide along with them.

I accept that only other species are able to get close to me.

I will nurture all of my anxieties and
fears on this day.

❧

I delight in my ability to pout and sulk.

Summer's happy blossoms taunt me as
I dwell in my drab little world.

Today I will judge my partner
on glorified remembrances of a
long-since withered relationship.

$\mathcal{T}$oday I will drink so much coffee I will give myself an anxiety attack.

❧

$\mathcal{B}$y forcing myself to smile brilliantly when I really feel like crying hysterically, I will eventually be able to circumvent all "bad" emotions.

I accept that I am a humorless wretch.

❧

When I get bored at work today,
I will verbally abuse an underling.

$\mathcal{T}$oday I will casually bring up
a controversial issue with a friend and
then act self-righteously if he or she
doesn't agree with me.

❧

$\mathcal{I}$ will make fun of others who aren't
like me today.

Today I celebrate the knowledge
that I have never been, nor shall I
ever be, independent.

❦

My life is harder than everyone else's;
therefore, I deserve praise for
every little thing I do.

Other people's deliberate mistakes
sabotage me from achieving my goals.

❧

Touching is bad. Today I will remind
myself to shrink away if someone
wants physical contact.

I give myself permission to further obscure my identity.

❧

I will overextend myself today, making extravagant promises. I will then follow through on nothing.

$\mathcal{M}$y every desire, even if a momentary whim, should be fulfilled.

❦

$\mathcal{I}$t is more important for me to perservate on my own problems than it is for me to be aware of current world events.

Today I will practice the art of denial.

It is never okay to ask for help.
I must do everything on my own to
ensure it is done correctly.

$\mathcal{D}$reams are for weaklings who
can't deal with reality.

❧

$\mathcal{M}$y house is the only safe place
in my life.

There is no room in my life for detours;
I must always stick to my original plan.

❧

Control of my life exists externally
from myself; today I seek to determine
its exact origin.

Today I will be rigid and withholding.

As I have worked long and hard
to polish my skill of feeling sorry for
myself, today I will recognize that
accomplishment.

$\mathcal{T}$oday I will access my desire to
be perfect as a way of enabling myself to
thrive in my overly rigid lifestyle.

❧

$\mathcal{I}$ will blame someone else for all
that goes wrong today.

Tonight I will awaken at 3 A.M., at which
point I will obsess about my finances.

Today I will invalidate a friend
who is in therapy by telling him or her
it is just a crutch.

Today I will pick a beautiful bouquet
of flowers out of someone's yard,
without permission.

✎

Today I will practice walking and
carrying myself like a victim.

I will make it a point to sigh heavily at certain times today, then deny anything is wrong when people ask.

If other people did the emotional work they needed to, they would be better able to deal with my cruelty.

To squelch my fear of abandonment,
I will make sure to thwart my children's
efforts to grow into separate beings.

Today I will scoff at people,
like my boss, who think they know
more than I do.

*I*nstead of confronting people who anger me, I will get back at them by doing nasty things to them in my fantasies.

*B*ecause no one likes to be around a nuisance, I must remind myself to be as convenient and malleable as possible.

$\mathcal{T}$oday I will drown my sorrows by charging gifts for myself.

_∽_

$\mathcal{T}$oday I will return the gifts I bought for myself. I will then get in touch with my resentment for not being financially privileged.

It is more important to have a perfectly clean house and weedless lawn than it is to protect myself or the environment from harsh chemicals.

I will get so upset today that I will make myself physically ill, which will allow me to rest without guilt.

$\mathcal{T}$oday I will brighten up my usually dismal life by pretending everyone is jealous of my beauty and talent.

❧

$\mathcal{T}$oday I will practice looking forlorn.

To get the attention I so rightly deserve, I will wear a ridiculous outfit today.

❧

Because the world we live in is wasteful and self-absorbed, I shouldn't have to be any better than that.

When someone in my family hurts me, I will picture him or her inconsolably sobbing at my funeral.

❧

I have a right to overheat my home so that all visitors stick to my plastic upholstery covers.

Although the holidays are still
months away, I will nurture a feeling
of dread today.

I will self-medicate myself today.

I have a right to be a victim after all
I have been through.

❧

Today I will allow my inner child
to frolic by playing a prank on
someone in pain.

· 113 ·

Today I will reconcile myself to the fact that no one's recovery is as difficult as mine.

Today I will focus on one aspect of my body that displeases me.

This week I will experiment with how long I can go without sleep before it starts impairing my judgment.

I am aging very poorly.

The next time I see an especially
suspenseful movie, I must remind myself
to use the knowledge I gain to spoil
it for someone who hasn't seen it.

᷍

Today I will ruminate on the fact that
my higher power has abandoned me.

$\mathcal{I}$ will eat compulsively today.

❧

$\mathcal{I}$ have a right to seek out
inappropriate sex partners.

Today I will make detailed lists in my journal when others disappoint or anger me; later, I will throw it in their faces.

Today I will respect my need to sabotage everyone's success.

I must talk, talk, talk.
Otherwise, people will forget I'm around.

✑

I will only allow my pets to get close
to me, as they cannot hurt me.

Today I will make a new friend based solely on how he or she can further my career.

Today I will experiment with enmeshing myself with whomever I deem worthy.

$\mathcal{S}$ince being alone is too threatening
for me, I will surround myself
with people regardless of whether or
not I like them.

❦

$\mathcal{I}$t is okay for me to read other
people's mail when I feel suspicious, as
long as I cover my tracks by acting
shocked that it's opened.

Today I seek clarity—I will ask for my family's agenda for me in writing.

I am heartily ashamed of my past and who it has shaped me into.

$\mathcal{P}$arental war crimes, except those
I may inadvertently commit, should
never be forgiven.

❧

$\mathcal{I}$ take pride in the fact that
I have never, nor will I ever, share my
feelings with anyone.

I have a right to financially
and emotionally suck my parents dry.

❧

I look to each day with dread and
apprehension.

Today I will act on a paranoid thought.

❦

Today I will scare myself by visualizing
bad things happening to me.

Since I have a right to hold grudges, I also have a right to spread false rumors.

Today I will practice being defiant in all my interactions with others.

$\mathcal{T}$oday I will patronize an
authority figure.

❧

$\mathcal{T}$oday I will pick out one physical flaw
in everyone I see.

$\mathcal{T}$oday I will remind myself that
I never make mistakes.

❧

$\mathcal{S}$urrounding myself with emotional
weaklings is a valid way to protect my
individuality.

My problems are more severe than
everyone else's and, therefore,
deserve top priority.

∽

If I was a member of the opposite sex,
life would be much simpler.

I am not responsible and should never
be treated as such.

✍

I have a right to whine in order to
get my needs met first.

$\mathcal{T}$oday I accept the necessity
of controlling the inferior people
around me.

$\mathcal{S}$

$\mathcal{C}$reativity is for naive,
shallow people.

$\mathcal{P}$rocrastination is a safe and effective way to deal with decisions.

❧

$\mathcal{T}$oday I will use chocolate to fill my empty, inner wasteland.

I accept my right to be stagnant.

∽

Because I have such a frenzied life,
I will purposely cut in line today.

Since I am unable to meet my own needs, I will make a point of staying in unhealthy relationships.

Because my lover's appearance is a direct reflection on me, I have a right to demand that he or she exercise.

$\mathcal{I}$ will teach others to avoid conflict today, as it was avoided in my family while I was growing up.

$\mathcal{T}$oday I will minimize my feelings, wants, and needs.

$\mathcal{P}$essimism is the only practical,
realistic way to look at life.

$\mathcal{T}$oday I allow myself to be
guided by greed.

Today I will dwell in the
there and then.

❧

The next time I want attention, I will
intentionally load my grocery cart with
unpriced items that are on special.

Today I will nurture my feelings of
hatred toward others.

I will second guess myself as much
as possible today.

$\mathcal{T}$oday I will pick on an underdog.

❦

$\mathcal{I}$ will start today by reminding myself
that I used to be a lot younger,
thinner, and happier.

Today I will talk to my inner child using only "shoulds" and "have-to's."

❧

The people who have hurt me in the past hold the key to my future.

$\mathcal{B}$ecause I demand that everything
in my life is the best and most beautiful,
I will disown my body today.

⟂

$\mathcal{M}$oney is more important than
love or friends.

Today the fall leaves remind me of the importance of life's processes.
Death is inevitable.

Since no one seems willing
to take responsibility for anything,
it is best for me to take responsibility
for everything.

$\mathcal{A}$s I have no tolerance for silence,
I will invest in a new, high-tech
entertainment center today.

$\mathcal{S}$elf-pity is the stuff from
which life is made.

Today I will loan a bothersome friend
a novel with pivotally important
pages removed.

❧

Today I will question my own authority.

Tonight, by moonlight, I will rake my leaves into my neighbor's yard.

✧

I have a right to belong nowhere.

The next time I get tired of
name-calling or doubt its effectiveness,
I will switch to the more sophisticated
technique of using pop psychology
to judge others.

The next time I eat at a restaurant,
I will passively accept even the
lousiest service.

Today I will sign my child up for
music, dance, or sports lessons
that I wish I had taken as child but for
which my child shows no inclination.

⁂

I have a right to enable others in their
compulsive behaviors.

Although I understand that I must
walk through the pain, not around it,
I affirm my right to do so
in a medicated state.

❧

I am inherently abnormal.

Today I will ignore my inner child.

❦

This morning I will deal with my
physical unattractiveness by dressing
in drab, baggy clothing.

$\mathcal{I}$ accept that I am alienated from life's continuum.

❧

$\mathcal{T}$oday I will inflict guilt upon others if they do not live up to my expectations.

Today I will set someone else up
for failure.

❧

Today I will research an obscure
historical event. Later I will refer to it in
conversation, acting judgmentally
when no one knows of it.

$\mathcal{T}$oday I will punish a loved one for a past disappointment.

⚜

$\mathcal{T}$oday I will terrorize my inner child.

Today at work, I will take credit for something I didn't do.

❧

Today I will continually seek approval from everyone around me.

I have no need to resolve the wounds
of my past; I am most comfortable
surrounded by a cloak of denial.

I must remind myself today that
it is always too late to have a
happy childhood.

Although a lot of people are talking about ACOA issues, recovery, etc., they still wouldn't understand my pain.

I take pride in the fact that my personal power comes from my innate sense of insecurity.

I accept that I am an abusive parent
to my inner child.

❧

I will begin this day by looking at an
old photo album to prove that gravity is
having quite an effect on me.

I will remind myself today that I need
no one. I am an island.

✍

I am alienated from the earth, sky,
and universe.

$\mathcal{I}$ affirm my right to trust no one and rely only on myself.

❧

$\mathcal{T}$oday I will make peace with someone who I'm not speaking to so I can borrow money.

$\mathcal{I}$f another person rejects me,
it is because of his or her
deep-seated problems.

❧

$\mathcal{T}$oday I will taunt others until they cry,
then tell them they are too sensitive.

If someone compliments me today,
I will look for the hidden agenda.

It is reasonable to demand that my true
friends grow and change at the same
rate, and in the same way, as I do.

*I*n the holiday spirit,
I will take a rich dessert to work today
and tell everyone it's fat-free.

❧

I have a right to persistently
complain about the results of elections
in which I haven't voted.

Today I will read about a strange disease;
I will then spend the day tracing
my symptoms.

Today I will reconcile myself
to the fact that the world really is
pitted against me.

$\mathcal{B}$ecause the only physical comfort
I receive comes from my afghan,
today I will lie in bed all day.

$\mathcal{T}$oday I will practice using the
word *pathetic* in reference to
other people and their lives.

So that I can recklessly abandon all measures of restraint on Thanksgiving Day, I will starve myself today.

Today I will come up with derisive code names for my neighbors.

$\mathcal{I}$ will envy others today.

❧

$\mathcal{T}$oday I will remind myself that
there is no light at the end of
the tunnel. This is how my life
will always be.

Today I will purposefully
not do something that would make
a friend happy.

Today I will remind one of my parents
how he or she abused and/or neglected
me as a child.

Today I will suppress my feelings.

⚬

Today I will reacquaint myself with
my childhood playmates:
loneliness and pain.

Although I find the holiday season difficult and am often disappointed, today I will employ my time-proven methods of building false expectations.

Today I will invalidate the feelings and perceptions of those around me.

Today I will acknowledge my
inherent shame and try to be as
inconspicuous as possible.

I accept that without pain or regret,
I would be emotionally numb.

$\mathcal{I}$ have a right to act out
in harmful ways.

❧

$\mathcal{T}$oday I will practice new ways of
expressing my impatience.

To be prepared, today I will spend time
fabricating an exciting tale to tell
at a holiday party.

❧

Today I will put undue pressure on
myself to be the best.

Today I will blame a coworker
for a mistake I made.

❧

If I get lonely today,
I will call mail-order catalogs and place
false, but elaborate orders.

All of my problems must be solved
at once . . . immediately.

❧

It is okay to lie as long
as it benefits me in the long run.

Most likely my sexuality is perverse;
I had best keep it to myself.

⚬

Today I will overwork myself to
test my limits.

*I*nstead of spending my hard-earned
cash on presents for my family,
I will give them things I am tired of or
that I've broken.

❧

*T*oday I will think about past losses and
plan ways to avoid them in the future.

Feelings are overrated and should
be denied at all times.

❦

Today I will see the bad in everything so
as not to get my hopes up.

I have a right to disrespect others.

❧

I must remind myself that winning is
the only thing that counts, and losing is
for complete and utter failures.

My self-worth is based on
my accomplishments; therefore, I must
do as much as I can in a short
period of time.

❦

I am inherently untrustworthy.

My needs are more important than
other people's needs.

❧

I am at peace with nothing.

$\mathcal{T}$oday I will equate material possessions with love.

❧

$\mathcal{F}$amilies are the root of all evil and should be avoided at all costs.

$\mathcal{I}$ will remind myself today that the emotion of fear is only for children.

❧

$\mathcal{I}$ have a right to abuse people who want to show their feelings.

I have a right to display
inappropriate anger.

❦

Today I will act superior to others.

Today I will look back on the year and remind myself how perfect I am in comparison to others.

$\mathcal{D}$o you have a cynical affirmation
you would like to share ?

If so, send it to:

Sarah Wells and Ann Thornhill
C/O Prima Publishing
3875 Atherton Road
Rocklin, CA 95765

Please note: Prima Publishing may want to
publish your cynical affirmation along with
your name in a future version of this book. By
submitting a response, you agree that Prima
shall own all rights in the cynical affirmation,
including the right to publish the affirmation
and give credit to you as the author of the
affirmation.